Contents

Any words appearing in the text in bold, **like this**, are explained in the Glossary.

What do goldfish look like?

A goldfish is a type of fish that lives in cold water. Most goldfish have a shiny orange skin. They have tails and **fins** to help them swim through water.

Goldfish come in different shapes and sizes.

A Pet's Life

Goldfish

Anita Ganeri

www.heinemannlibrary.co.uk
Visit our website to find out more information about Heinemann Library books.

To order:

 Phone +44 (0) 1865 888066

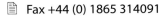 Fax +44 (0) 1865 314091

 Visit www.heinemannlibrary.co.uk

Heinemann Library is an imprint of Capstone Global Library Limited, a company incorporated in England and Wales having its registered office at 7 Pilgrim Street, London, EC4V 6LB – Registered company number: 6695582

"Heinemann" is a registered trademark of Pearson Education Limited, under licence to Capstone Global Library Limited.

Edited by Charlotte Guillain and Harriet Milles
Designed by Joanna Hinton-Malivoire
Picture research by Liz Alexander
Production by Victoria Fitzgerald
Originated by Chroma Graphics (Overseas) Pte. Ltd
Printed and bound in China by South China Printing Company Ltd.

ISBN 978 0431 1 7789 2 (hardback)
13 12 11 10 09
10 9 8 7 6 5 4 3 2 1

ISBN 978 0 4311 7796 0 (paperback)
13 12 11 10 09
10 9 8 7 6 5 4 3 2 1

British Library Cataloguing in Publication Data
Ganeri, Anita, 1961-
   Goldfish. - 2nd ed. - (A pet's life) (Heinemann first library)
   1. Goldfish - Juvenile literature
   I. Title
   639.3'7484
A full catalogue record for this book is available from the British Library.

Acknowledgements
We would like to thank the following for permission to reproduce photographs:
Alamy pp. **5** (© Eureka), **26** (© Sami Sarkis Images); © Capstone Global Library Ltd. pp. **27** (Aylesbury Studios), **8**, **12**, **14**, **15**, **16**, **17**, **19**, **22**, **24**, **25** (Haddon Davies), **10**, **11**, **13**, **18** (Tudor Photography); Corbis pp. **9** (© Michael Keller), **20** (© DK Limited), **21** (© Michael Boys); Dave Bevan p. **23**; Dorling Kindersley pp. **6**, **7** (Neil Fletcher); Photolibrary p. **4** (Juniors Bildarchiv).

Cover photograph of goldfish reproduced with permission of Photolibrary (Juniors Bildarchiv).

The publishers would like to thank Rob Lee for his assistance in the preparation of this book.

Every effort has been made to contact copyright holders of material reproduced in this book. Any omissions will be rectified in subsequent printings if notice is given to the publishers.

This picture shows the different parts of a goldfish's body. You can see what each part is used for.

Tail for steering and pushing.

Smooth body for swimming.

Scaly skin for protection.

Eyes for seeing.

Fins for steering, braking, and balancing.

Gills for taking in **oxygen** from the water.

Mouth for gulping in water and food.

5

Goldfish babies

Goldfish **hatch** from eggs. The female lays thousands of eggs in the water. The eggs are sticky and look like blobs of jelly.

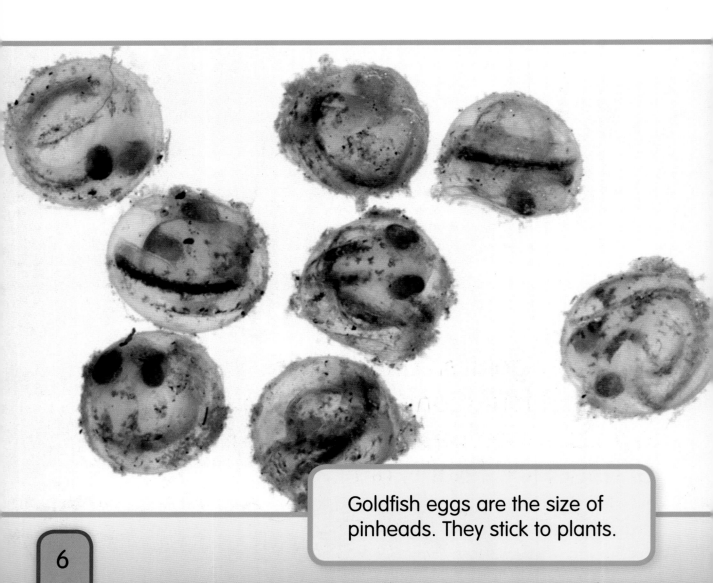

Goldfish eggs are the size of pinheads. They stick to plants.

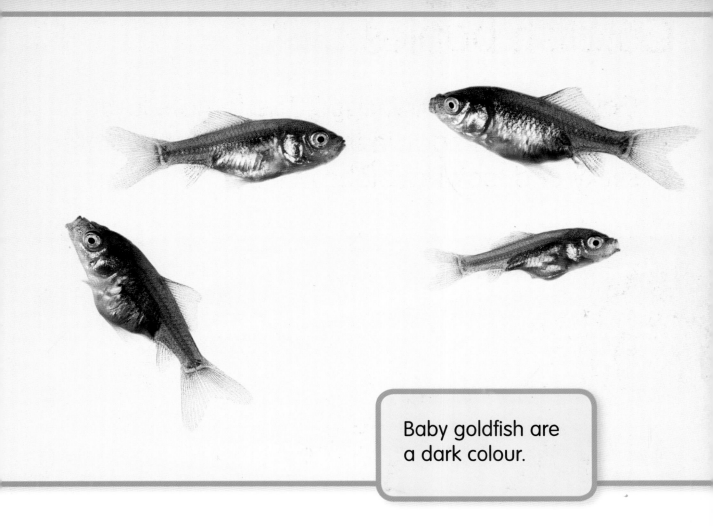

Baby goldfish are a dark colour.

The baby goldfish are called fry. It takes the fry about four months to grow into adult goldfish. Their bodies become shiny orange at about six months old.

Choosing your goldfish

You can buy your goldfish from a good pet shop, a garden centre, or from a fish-keeper's club.

Before you buy any fish, check that they are healthy.

Choose a fish with bright, clear eyes and shiny skin. It should not be slow-moving, or have split or damaged **fins**. If the fish looks like this, it may be unwell.

A healthy fish should be active with upright fins.

Setting up your tank

Your fish need a tank to live in. A tank that measures 90 x 38 x 30 cm will have room for five to eight small fish.

Place your tank out of bright sunlight and draughts.

You need to fill the tank with water but you must mix tap water with special liquids first. Put **gravel** and stones in the bottom to make it interesting for your fish.

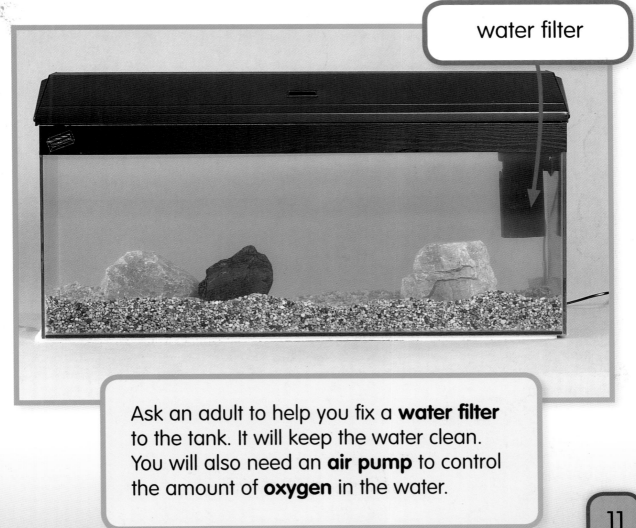

water filter

Ask an adult to help you fix a **water filter** to the tank. It will keep the water clean. You will also need an **air pump** to control the amount of **oxygen** in the water.

Putting in plants

It is a good idea to put some water plants into your tank. You can dig small holes in the **gravel** and push the plants in.

There are lots of different types of water plants. Ask your pet shop to help you choose the best plants for your tank.

Plants are useful because they make **oxygen** for your fish to breathe. Your fish will also like to swim among their leaves.

You can cover your tank with a hood that has a light.

Welcome home

You can carry your fish home in a plastic bag of water. You should float the bag of goldfish in your tank for 20 minutes.

If you tip your fish straight into the tank, the different water **temperatures** may shock your goldfish and make them ill.

Make sure that the water temperature in the bag is the same as in the tank. Then you can let your goldfish out of the bag.

If you need to move your fish, do not touch them with your hands. Use a net or jug.

Feeding time

You can buy special goldfish food from a pet shop. You can also give your fish some chopped lettuce or spinach leaves.

Special fish flakes give your fish the goodness they need.

Watch your fish swim to the surface to gobble up their food.

Feed your fish once a day. Take care not to give your fish too much food. It can turn bad and **poison** the water.

Cleaning the tank

It is important to take care of the tank to keep your fish healthy. Your goldfish will quickly become ill in a dirty tank. Every day, check that the water is clean. About every ten days, clean the entire tank.

Clean any green **slime** off the inside of the glass with a special sponge.

Take out half of the old water. Put this water into a bucket and place your goldfish in the bucket. Clean the tank and the gravel thoroughly. Fill up the tank with clean water and put the goldfish back in.

You can use a **siphon tube** to take some water out of your tank.

Growing up

Goldfish get bigger as they grow into adults. Watch how big your fish grow and make sure that your tank does not get overcrowded.

Fish that are about 7 cm long are the best size for your tank.

If you have a garden, you might be able to make your own pond.

If your goldfish grow longer than 12 cm, they should live in an outside pond. Goldfish can grow very big in a pond. Never put goldfish into rivers or streams.

Healthy goldfish

Goldfish will stay healthy if you care for them properly. Check your goldfish every day. If you think your goldfish looks ill, call your **vet**.

The vet will be able to tell you what is wrong with your goldfish.

If a fish is ill, it is best to move it into a separate tank until it is better.

If a fish seems to be moving slowly, it may not be well. Drooping **fins** or white spots on its skin are also signs of illness.

Your pet goldfish

Goldfish make great pets and are fun to keep. But you must be a good pet owner and care for them properly.

Your goldfish will depend on you for all their needs.

If you go away on holiday, make sure that someone looks after your goldfish. Ask a friend or neighbour to call in every day.

Always make sure that your goldfish have the right food and that their tank is clean.

Old age

If you look after your goldfish well, they can live for many years. They do not need any special care as they get older.

A common goldfish can live for up to 25 years!

Caring for your fish will help you learn how to treat animals properly.

It can be very upsetting when your pet dies. Try not to be too sad. Just remember all the happy times that you shared.

Useful tips

- Wash your hands before and after you clean out the tank or feed your fish.

- Never tap the glass of the tank. This will annoy or shock your fish.

- Always keep the tank covered and out of reach of cats and other pets.

- Leave your fish to settle in for two weeks before you add any more.

- When you are cleaning out the tank, put your fish in some of the old water in a bucket.

- Never keep your fish in a goldfish bowl. There will not be enough **oxygen** for them to breathe.

Fact file

- Goldfish were first kept as pets by Chinese people over 4,500 years ago.

- The oldest goldfish on record was thought to be 49 years old when it died.

- Some common goldfish can grow to about 40 cm long.

- Not all goldfish are orange. Some are yellow, red, black, white, or even blue. Some are a mix of all these colours.

- A female goldfish lays 1,000–3,000 eggs at a time.

- Many "fancy" types of goldfish have been bred, with features such as trailing fins or upturned eyes.

Glossary

air pump machine fixed to a fish tank to put oxygen into the water for your fish to breathe

fins flaps of skin that grow on a fish's body

gills parts of a fish's body that take oxygen from the water so the fish can breathe

gravel tiny stones

hatch when baby fish come out of their eggs

oxygen gas that animals need to breathe to stay alive

poison something that causes illness or death

slime thin, green film that forms on the tank

siphon tube piece of tube that can pull water upwards

temperature how hot or cold something is

water filter machine fixed to the side of the fish tank to keep the water clean

vet specially trained animal doctor

More information

Books to read

A First Look at Animals: Pets, Claire Watts (Two-Can, 2000)

Read and Learn: Goldfish, Jennifer Blizin Gillis (Heinemann Library, 2004)

RSPCA Pet Guide: Care for your Goldfish (Collins, 2004)

Websites

www.rspca.org.uk
The website of The Royal Society for the Prevention of Cruelty to Animals in Britain.

www.pethealthcare.co.uk
Information about keeping and caring for pets.

www.petlink.com.au
Information about being a good pet owner.

Index